CONFESS *to* STRESS

CONFESS to STRESS

*A Christian Teacher's Approach
to Defeating Stress*

KYLE TAFT

Illustrated by: Kelsea Taft

WESTBOW
PRESS
A DIVISION OF THOMAS NELSON

Scripture taken from the King James Version of the Bible.

WestBow Press books may be ordered through booksellers or by contacting:

WestBow Press
A Division of Thomas Nelson
1663 Liberty Drive
Bloomington, IN 47403
www.westbowpress.com
1 (866) 928-1240

ISBN: 978-1-4908-1667-8 (sc)
ISBN: 978-1-4908-1666-1 (hc)
ISBN: 978-1-4908-1668-5 (e)

Library of Congress Control Number: 2013921037

Printed in the United States of America.

WestBow Press rev. date: 12/09/2013

To my wonderful wife, Patty, for helping me
make it through this most stressful process of
writing a book about dealing with stress!

To Kaitlyn, my youngest daughter, for patiently leaving
the office each time I told her I couldn't do whatever
she had asked because I was working on my book.

To Kelsea, my oldest daughter, who in spite of the
challenges of graduating from high school, looking
for a job, and choosing a college, found the time
to sketch the illustrations here in this work.

Most of all: to my Lord and Savior Jesus Christ! Without Him
and His Holy Word, none of this would have meaning!

Contents

FOREWORD

By Joey Dean

When Kyle first mentioned he was working on a book, I was excited and very interested. When he asked me to write the foreword for *Confess to Stress*, I was honored. I have known Kyle for as long as I remember. We were both raised in a preacher's home (and no, not all preachers' kids are the worst), we both pursued careers in education, and we both currently serve as pastors. These similarities have contributed to a strong friendship between us. Kyle has always been easy to talk to and offered sound advice. In this book, Kyle compiles some of the thoughts he has shared with me and others.

As a teacher, I felt the all too familiar pressure involved with the job. Now, as a pastor, I see the effects of stress in the people I counsel and in my own life. The simple truth is that stress is a part of almost everyone's life and that stress can have negative consequences.

While the target audience for *Confess to Stress* is teachers, the concepts work for almost any situation. I found it easily applicable to every facet of my life. Even if you have little or no experience in the field of education, I am certain that you will benefit from reading this book.

Kyle is not the first writer to tackle the issue of stress. I think, however, that Kyle's simple, straight forward, and biblically sound approach to the topic is fresh and relevant. As you read, I trust that you will find it as helpful as I did. In it you will find the inspiration to cope with your stress.

Preface

With all of the materials already in print dealing with stress, why would I be crazy enough to attempt writing yet another? No doubt millions of dollars have been spent trying to find the answers to the problems we say are caused by stress. I can assure you that I did not just wake up one morning with the thought, "Hey, I am going to write a book about stress!" It was rather a process that took place over the course of a couple of years.

It started at Temple Calvary Holiness Church, a small country church in rural South Georgia that I pastored for twelve years. Not only am I involved in education, first as an elementary school teacher and now as a college professor, but several in my congregation are teachers, principals, lunchroom workers, etc. One, a principal of an elementary school, approached me about coming to speak to his teachers before returning to the classroom following a break. His reason was that they were in need of some motivation after going through a series of stressful changes at their school. Since I was all too familiar with the stresses of a classroom, I agreed to come and try to help. After much prayer and meditation, I presented an uplifting and mostly humorous talk on teacher stress.

A few months later (I am not sure if someone from the school told them, or if they were just desperate), Bright from the Start, Georgia's licensing agency for childcare facilities, asked me to present my materials in a teacher training session. I agreed and travelled three and a half hours to deliver an hour talk about teacher stress. When I arrived, I found that none of my requested equipment was there. Needless to say, it was a stressful afternoon! However, due to the topic of my presentation I remained calm, made some quick adjustments, and we had a great meeting.

Soon thereafter, I was honored to be added to the list of presenters at the 2012 Georgia Preschool Association Conference in Atlanta. It was there, after presenting two sessions of around one hundred teachers each, I was given the idea of turning my thoughts into a book. On the second day, a teacher came to me after the session and asked if I had a book out. When I replied in the negative, she suggested I write one. Her reason was that she had many teacher friends who needed to hear this message.

As I gave it some thought, I realized that most teachers probably go through the same levels of stress that she was experiencing. Then I thought about others who are not teachers, but are also in stressful situations in their careers. I began to pray and seek guidance from God. As a result, I felt His nudge, letting me know that I should go ahead and give it a shot. I have poured my heart into this work. My hope and prayer is that it will touch many, and bring new perspective to some lives. However, if one person is all it ever reaches, if just one life is changed from reading this book, it will be worth every minute I have spent pecking on this keyboard! May God richly bless you and speak to your heart as you read.

Introduction

S tress. This simple word seems to be the cause of every problem, situation, health issue, or mental breakdown faced by today's families. How many times in a conversation does the word "stress" come up? If a person's blood pressure is rising, they will tell everyone it is due to stress. If one develops a bad attitude with the spouse or kids, it is okay, because it is stress. Being too stressed is why most people have heart attacks. At least that is what I have heard. People are even blaming their nervous breakdowns on stress. In fact, stress has caused so many maladies that it seems everywhere you turn, you see some new way to combat stress.

There are "stress relief" workouts at the local gym. (Of course, they are now open all night to accommodate your stressful and busy days.) You can take yoga classes, dance lessons, and relaxation seminars. You can learn to breathe right, eat right, sleep right, and think right. You can meditate, participate, rededicate, and vacate. You can even go to the herbal store and medicate. All of these processes are "guaranteed" your stress to eradicate.

For teachers, stress is a very real problem that all too often goes unaddressed. In fact, teaching is one of the most stressful occupations in the world, along with air traffic controllers, police officers, and firefighters. Many may contend that this statement is ridiculous. However, I am a teacher and have also served as a firefighter for nineteen years. I can tell you from experience that facing a burning building is sometimes easier and more routine than facing twenty second graders on the first day of school.

Think about it. A fire in a home or office is somewhat predictable. You know how to ventilate the roof to cause the flames to move towards the oxygen supply. You can concentrate on the immediate task at hand, because you have a partner with you who is watching your back. You have gallons and gallons of water at your disposal, and there are people on the outside whose sole purpose is to make sure you continue to be supplied with everything you need. Simply follow the rules of safety, do what you have been taught, and soon you will gain the upper hand against the fire.

On the other hand, walk into the classroom. Twenty pairs of eyes stare at you. Behind each pair sits a fascinating brain. That gives you twenty brains working independently of each other. Each brain is capable of creating total chaos and confusion with little more than a thought and can accomplish just that without consulting with any other brain

Oh, what a fascinating brain!

in the room. What makes the situation worse is that you never know which brain will erupt next. In fact, it is that one brain that has not performed an unusual act in years that is going to turn your classroom upside down next. No amount of training can ever prepare you for these unexpected moments in the classroom. Sure, you will have those great and uneventful days, but teachers always know that at any given time anything can happen.

Your educational instructors taught you in college that you must always be prepared for the unexpected and the unknown. If you think about that statement, your stress level will go through the roof. How are you supposed to prepare for the unknown? How can you expect the unexpected? Better yet, how can you even begin to prepare for something you know nothing about? So teachers run around frantically preparing for every possible incident, only to find that the one thing they did not imagine is the very thing that happened today. Why do you think there are so many diverse classroom management strategies on the market? It is because we are constantly discovering contingencies that we did not plan for.

To make matters even more stressful, as you gaze at the twenty darlings assigned to you, it suddenly occurs to you that you are alone. I can remember being so excited about getting my first classroom and then panicking on the first day of school because it was my classroom. Then all of the teachers who were so encouraging during the year's pre-planning meetings and even offered their assistance, are now in their classrooms, staring with fear at their own collection of twenty different brains. Unlike in my example of the firefighter earlier, there are no endless supplies of the things you need to help you. Each "fire" in your classroom is different, and you must instantly figure out the best way to control every one. Not only do you have to keep the students safe, you have to entertain them, doctor them, console them, counsel them, control them, and somehow educate them. No wonder teaching is considered one of the most stressful occupations in the world!

I have read many studies on teacher stress. While most of the results vary drastically, one result is consistent. This disturbing trend is that there are a lot of new teachers entering the classroom, becoming great teachers, and then changing their careers within the first five years of teaching. Each teacher I know who has done this cited stress and burnout as the cause for their change. Therefore, we can conclude that many of our trained and highly qualified teaching professionals are being lost because of the unending stress of the classroom. Rest assured that children's natural tendencies will never be changed, so the only other option is to approach this problem of stress. Surely the loss of so many great teachers would cause those in charge to desire to diligently look for a way to alleviate this issue. Obviously, the many strategies mentioned earlier have not been successful. We need a new approach.

In this book, I would like to offer a new – yet as old as the world – and innovative alternative to the standard remedies for stress. The reality is stress can be controlled. However, it is not something that needs medicine, dieting, exercise, and psychiatrists. Those strategies are effective, but they relieve only the symptoms of stress. They treat the outward manifestations of a bigger problem. The truth is that we have caused ourselves to be stressed. The symptoms that show on the outside are really just the evidence of something more deeply rooted on the inside. I propose to show you four biblical principles that will address these problems and help change you on the inside. Then, when the inside is changed, stress will leave, you will be more relaxed, and your symptoms will disappear!

I will be the first to tell you that I am not an expert. I do not have a PhD in the study of psychological emotional issues. I have not poured over years and years of research regarding this topic. However, what I do have to offer you is experience. I have been in the classroom, standing in front of the students thinking, "Okay, now what?" I have had the behavior problems. I have dealt with the defiant parents. I had to stop one mother from leaving with her son during a tornado (this was not a drill), and was threatened with a lawsuit as a result. I have been physically attacked by a student. I have broken up fights. I have had a little girl confide to me that someone in her family had been touching her. I have had a legal guardian come to a parent/teacher conference drunk. I have been physically threatened by an irate dad. I have been cursed out by a ticked off mom. I have had a student's dad get arrested for DUI. I have had a student's house burn down during the school day. I have been pressured by a principal to change a child's grade (no lie). I have had students with Asperger's, Tourette's, autism, emotional and behavioral disorders, attention-deficit disorder, attention-deficit/hyperactivity disorder, hearing impairments, asthma, mental delays, severe allergies, and those who spoke English as a second language. Then I have had students who were just plain bad! So I speak from experience.

How have I managed to stay sane? How have I dealt with the stress? I will admit there have been many times when I started to join the ranks of the career changers. However, I have found that the strategies outlined in this book have always helped to keep me focused. The psalmist David said it best when he instructed his friends, "When my heart is overwhelmed: lead me to the Rock that is higher than I" (Psalm 61:2). That is what I want my focus to be in the pages of this little book. I want to bring to your attention to the fact that there are eternal principles that can and will alleviate your feelings of stress if you will follow them.

My desire has been to write this as though we were having a conversation over a cup of coffee. This has thrown the editing staff into a panic. Their job is to make sure every sentence has the perfect structure and that every word is grammatically correct. However, I am not writing a formal textbook. I pray and believe that those who read this will hear my voice. Teachers especially will understand why I have written the way I have. Too much editing changes what I am trying to say and the voice becomes someone else's. This is me. All of the structural mistakes are mine. Some are intentional. Some may not be. Either way, I am serious about our conversation. When you read, you will be getting me, my heart, and nothing else.

With that said, I acknowledge that this book is written for teachers, but the strategies are about life in general. They can be applied to any profession. So if you are not a teacher, please do not put this book down. I think you will find stress relief for your life as well. Now, sit back, relax, and follow me to a less stressful career and life.

CHAPTER ONE
WHAT IS STRESS ANYWAY?

The Search For Truth

I really wanted to do some viable research for this book, so I began to search for a solid definition or explanation for stress. Unfortunately, I found that despite thousands of experts, no one can agree about what stress really is. Even the evidence from countless studies and hours of research seems to say it has all been a fruitless attempt to solve the mystery of stress. As I looked at more and more research, I found myself coming to the conclusion that the more we discover about stress, the less we can explain it. So for years, psychiatrists, doctors, lawyers, yoga instructors, and health food gurus have made millions of dollars trying to treat something they can't even explain. How then can something that is so unexplainable be used to explain so much? Another question would be, if someone cannot accurately define and explain stress, then how can there be so many so-called remedies?

So, what is stress anyway? Well, it would seem that the correct definition depends on which group you listen to. First, some professionals declare that stress is a chemical imbalance in the brain. Their explanation is that the brain becomes saturated with too many chemicals or hormones at the same time, and this causes unnatural behaviors of the physical body and the person's emotions become infected. Why call it an infection? Well, isn't that what an infection is: a substance that should not be in the body which causes unnatural behaviors in the body and its emotional system? If this is true, then we should be able to prescribe some type of medication to counteract the effects of these chemicals. So these professionals, based on their explanation of symptoms and diagnosis of the stress disease, are all about treating stress with another foreign substance going into the body and possibly triggering unnatural behaviors in the body and its emotional system.

So, let's consider the possibilities of taking medication for the alleviation of stress. Have you ever listened to the possible side effects of these stress medications? They fall under many titles, and are almost all guaranteed to help you relax; if only you can deal with the nausea, vomiting, diarrhea, headaches, dizziness, and fainting spells. Don't forget that while you relax, you may feel the sudden urge to yell at your family and kick the children's dog. I have even heard warnings that the stress relief drugs may cause heightened feelings of depression and one commercial said that their pill may cause thoughts of suicide! Do I really think the tradeoff is worth it? Let's face it. Medication, except in extreme cases, is probably not the best choice for stress relief.

Other experts say that stress is caused by a person being so busy with life's many challenges that the body and brain become overwhelmed with all they are trying to accomplish. Looking at the fast paced society in which we now live, this seems to be a feasible diagnosis. It seems that there is never enough time in the day to complete that day's list. We run around frantically all day, and then collapse exhausted and drained. The problem must be, how do we slow down? What part of your life do you think you can give up? Just because you think you are too busy, do the deadlines stop looming? Does the paperwork suddenly complete itself when someone informs you that you are stressed?

Of course these experts say taking a few simple yoga classes will take care of this problem. If this is not an option, then the stressed individual should try a hobby, join a book club, or volunteer at a local charity. Although each of these may be interesting things to do, do they really bring relief from stress? The professional opinion is that we are too busy, and that busy lifestyle is what is causing us to be stressed. Is that so? Then, I guess it makes perfect sense that a professional would prescribe another activity to my schedule in order to relieve me of the stress caused by having too much on my schedule. Really!?! Seriously, I know a teacher that gets very stressed if she is running late for her scheduled time at the gym. Would that mean she is getting stressed over getting rid of stress?

Speaking of the gym; going there is a sure way to relieve stress. Is obesity a cause of stress, or does being under so much stress lead to obesity? I get it confused. Anyway, we need to join the health club or gym so we can diet and exercise. Surely those two activities (that I do not have time for) will help relieve my symptoms. The problem is though, when I diet, I want to eat everything that I am not supposed to have, so my stress level increases. Then when I exercise, I think of how much time I am wasting and get stressed.

Oh, I have got it! What we need is a week away for some rest and relaxation. Since that is your only week, however, you need to hurry, hurry, and hurry so you can go to every attraction. Then, when I am on a vacation, I worry about what I am missing back at the office, and my stress levels reach critical. Neither can I relax at home, because this book needs finishing, the yard needs mowing, the shrubs need trimming, the deck needs painting, the pool needs cleaning, the garden needs spraying, and those pesky armadillos are digging up my backyard again. The squirrels are shredding pinecones all over the yard, the deer have eaten my peas, and the neighbor's dog has left a gift piled right where I walk to my truck. Relax indeed!

So, let's go back to the original question. What is stress, anyway? After too much time spent with research (because I could have been doing something else), I finally ran across two wonderful explanations or definitions of stress. I could find no one to give credit to for these, but someone seemed to have great insight on stress. In fact, I believe every one of you can relate to these descriptions of stress.

The first quote took me a few minutes to comprehend. Think about this for a moment:

Stress is when you wake up screaming, only to realize you have never fallen asleep!

I can relate to this statement. Sometimes in life it seems everything that can possibly go wrong is going wrong at this very minute. You are so overwhelmed that one more thing will be the proverbial straw that breaks the camel's back. In your mind and in your heart you begin to believe that this has to be a dream. This is a nightmare. You literally scream in your dream and at that moment you realize that you are not dreaming. My friends, this is when stress is in overdrive!

The second definition of stress, and possibly my favorite, is easier to understand.

Stress is the confusion created when one's mind overrides the body's desire to choke the living daylights out of somebody who desperately needs it!

Have you ever had those thoughts? If you are a teacher and answered no to that question, you need to repent for lying! Either those children or their parents have driven you to this at some point in your career. So there you are. You are forcing that smile to appear on your face. You are speaking with a calm and relaxed voice. You remain ever the professional. But on the inside, the story is so different. On the inside, your brain is screaming at you to lash out. Your intellect is telling you what a dolt this person really is, and that someone should put them out of their misery. The movie screen in your mind is playing a fantasy of you getting your revenge for how you are being treated. There is a battle raging between your professionalism and teaching someone a lesson they really deserve. No wonder you are stressed.

The reason most of you are smiling right now is you know I am telling the truth. You know this because you are there. Your job has you over the barrel. The economy is driving you crazy, and you just went to the filling station and found that gas has gone up another fifty cents. Now, you have picked up a little book in hopes of trying to release some of your stress. Well, I do realize that wasting time is just going to add to your stress level, so I am not going to waste any more. I would like to invite you to come along on a quick journey of four simple steps that will relieve the stress in your life. Does that mean you will have no more situations that are unpleasant? No. Does it mean that you will never again feel the panic attacks rising up? No. Does it mean that you will never get angry and upset with people who just do not "get it"? No, of course it doesn't. What it does mean is that you will know exactly how to respond when those times do arise in your life.

CHAPTER TWO
S.T.A.
(STRESSED
TEACHERS
ANONYMOUS)

Admit It: Stress Has Got You!

I know I said there were only four steps to the recovery from stress. However, before you can begin that journey, you have to actually come to grips with the fact that you are stressed. We are in the teaching profession. It is a profession. That makes us professionals, right? Not only are we professionals, we are the professionals responsible for molding and shaping young minds to be the great leaders of tomorrow. With that in mind, we have no time to be stressed.

Think about it for a minute. We have the opportunity to open little minds to the greatness of the universe. Actually, it is more than just an opportunity. It is a responsibility. We can expose them to the magnificent world that we live in. We can begin an insatiable quest for knowledge, which may introduce mankind to the cure for cancer, the answer to economic woes, and the pathway to true peace. In fact, we teachers hold the key to this world's future in our hands every day. With so much power at our fingertips, there is no possible way we can be stressed. After all, teachers are obviously the most important people in the world.

On the other hand, this responsibility weighs heavily on our minds. Our success as teachers will bring us into a better world with a brighter future. However, what would our failure bring? A mail carrier fails on the route and delivers a letter to the wrong address. What are the consequences? There are none. Tomorrow, this worker simply picks up the failure and gets another attempt to make the correct delivery. This is no big deal, right? But when the teacher makes a mistake, it changes the course of the future. One misstep, one falter, one misplaced word, and the life of a child will be forever changed. No wonder you are stressed!

But teachers have many other reasons not to be stressed. If you think about the perks of the job, all of your stress should flee. Of course, there are the benefits afforded to all governmental employees. You have health care that costs nothing. You get at least one holiday per week. The workday does not begin until 9:00 in the morning, there are two breaks before lunch, an hour for that lunch, one afternoon break, and you get to go home at 3:30. All of your friends say, "Oh, if I could only have a job so easy. I mean, all you do at work is sit in a classroom with twenty kids and play." How could that be any less stressful?

However, my favorite perk is that we get summers off. Teachers only have to work nine months out of the year. Then they get to lie out on the beach or go to the mountains for the other three months. Did I mention that they draw a check while they are off those three months? Yes, I can hear you laughing as you read this. I have also heard some individuals make the statement that preschool "workers" are not really teachers. They just babysit a few babies. It would be funny to see them work with ten or twelve one year olds for just one day. Then on the other side of the age group, try controlling twenty twelfth graders for a day.

The fact is, you *are* stressed. You may think you are too much of a professional to be stressed, but I know. You are stressed. Let me just mention a few stressors that you face each day. First, there are the constant faculty meetings. Then you will attend your professional development workshops and more faculty meetings. We are implementing a new teaching strategy to our repertoire next week, so make sure you are at that training today at 4:00. Don't forget the SST meeting and that other faculty meeting. Also, we have planned an IEP meeting for little Johnny and just got an e-mail about another faculty meeting. Make sure your tiers of intervention are current, your grades are up to date, lesson plans are complete for the next three weeks, 504 plans are being implemented, room is ready for the AYP walk-through, Susie took her ADHD medicine after lunch, make at least two parent contacts today, and there is a faculty meeting at 3:00! Was that Billy that just threw up in the corner? Make sure you get that disinfected quickly. Oh that reminds me: at lunch we are going to have a quick grade-level discussion of this virus outbreak in the school. Did I mention the faculty meeting?

In the meantime, academic standings are low, and there is an ongoing search for the cause. So, teachers are being asked to implement every new teaching strategy that comes along. Nothing is given a chance to work. By the time you begin feeling comfortable with one thing, something new takes its place. Now with all of the new mandates from the United States Department of Education, standards are changing yet again. When does it stop?

Then, some well-meaning politician has decided that all of the educational problems are the fault of the teacher. It is all on you. So we implement a pay for performance standard for teachers. Teachers know that while this may sound like it will hold teachers accountable; it really creates a far worse problem. This pay for performance is based on the standardized test scores of students. With the advent of inclusion classrooms, teachers who are not special needs trained or certified are being held responsible for students that are mainstreamed into their classes who have learning disabilities. By using those students' scores on a pay for performance mandate, the temptation to cheat is made more prominent. The struggle between doing what is morally and ethically right and making sure their livelihood is preserved, compounds the level of stress teachers are facing each day.

To my non-teachers reading this book, I must say that though this sounds like I am making it up, I assure you, I am not. But your job is no different. You performed at 110% of production last week. You expected a congratulation of some sort. What you received, however, was an expectation of 115% this week. Your idea was laughed at. The dismal earnings report was totally your fault. I even had a manager tell me in one job that during breaks and lunches, I should perform my duties *and* those belonging to my partner in the same amount of time, while he was taking his break. So, I know that while you are not a teacher, you are under the same kind of pressure.

Now in order for any recovery program to be successful, you have to first admit that you have a problem and need help. All of us have a huge problem with that. It goes against every professional fiber in our being to admit that we are stressed. I guess to admit we cannot take the stress anymore, is to admit that we have a weakness! No one wants others to see them as weak! No one wants others to see them in pain. No one wants others to see them suffering, especially not a teacher. However, we all know that this is where recovery actually begins.

We can take all of the two-step, eight-step, and twelve-step plans we want. Yet until we realize that we have a problem, we will never desire help. Without ever desiring help, we will never be able to overcome our issues. It is really like the great plan of salvation. A sinner has to first come to the conclusion that he is a sinner. Then, he has to want a way out. Finally, to get out, he has to confess that he is guilty of sin! Without the confession of sin, there can be no forgiveness for the sin, or the eradication of it.

It is the same way with this "infection" of stress. You have to come to grips with the fact that you are indeed overly stressed. You have to have a desire to get some help and relief. If you are not willing to go that far, this book will be no more than a good, quick read (I hope) that has accomplished no more than entertain you for a moment. However, if you are sick and tired of being sick and tired, I invite you to enter the world of S.T.A., better known as Stressed Teachers Anonymous. In this world no one judges you, for we all have been at the same place you now sit. Really, though, there are only three people in this world of stress with you right now.

Obviously, you are here. Something about this title or something about this idea drew you to this place. Or maybe someone brought you here by giving you this book, because they realized what you may not: you are way too stressed. You know that you have been short with the spouse, hard on the kids, and have even threatened to kick the dog a time or two. Until now, you may have not even thought about why you are acting like this. It is stress. Therefore, since you are here, let the message of the book reach out to you.

Next, I am here with you. A burden has been placed on my heart to recognize and try to help you in your stress dilemma. There is no doubt in my mind that God put these words in my mouth in order to bring you to a brighter state of living. I was originally asked by an elementary school principal to give his teachers a little motivational pep talk as break was winding down. From there, I shared with classroom workers during an all-day Saturday training. Then I was asked to present this information to hundreds of teachers at an annual state conference. It was at that conference a teacher that I did not know asked me if I would consider writing this book. Her words were, "I know many teachers who need this desperately." So, what started out as an opportunity to touch a small group of teachers in rural South Georgia, has grown into a desire to help as many as I can, starting with you.

Finally, with us here, is the Ancient of Days. God is in this with you. He that knows more about you than you know about yourself is here and ready to help. As a matter of fact, He has already offered the first ever stress relief program. The ad ran like this: *"Come unto me, all ye that labour and are heavy laden and I will give you rest. Take my yoke upon you, and learn of me; for I am meek and lowly in heart: and ye shall find rest unto your souls. For my yoke is easy, and my burden light."* (Matthew 11:28 – 30) God knows that you face extraordinary pressure day in and day out. He knows that "things" pile up until you get overwhelmed. He wants to help you with that. He wants you to live stress free.

So the choice is yours. We have discussed what stress is. We have acknowledged that we need help with stress. Now, you must decide if you want the help. From here on out, this message is about getting out from under the stress that has you bound. Do you want that?

Before any of these steps can help you, you must do what the title of this book commands: "Confess to Stress!" You have to admit that you need help. So, if you seriously want help with your stress, go ahead and repeat after me: "My name is (state your name), and I AM STRESSED!"

CHAPTER THREE
LOOSEN UP!

I meet so many teachers (and people in general) who have forgotten how to smile. It seems that they are always mad about something, or acting as if someone has done them wrong. I have never seen as many people who are so pessimistic about seemingly everything. If you gave them a one hundred dollar bill, they would complain that it was too wrinkled! Why in the world are we so uptight about everything? Life is too short for us to waste time fretting about things we cannot change. So, the first step to fighting your stress is to loosen up!

To defeat this negative attitude that is permeating the teaching profession, we have to ask ourselves, "Why did I get into teaching anyway?" I believe the answer is the same for every teacher. The draw for going into a teaching career is not the money. Everyone knows that teachers do not make huge salaries. The pull is not the benefits. Although the benefits are great, they are not enough for the headache that comes with teaching. So, what is it that makes people decide to go into the teaching field?

Obviously, the answer to this question is the love of children. As we are making our decision to pursue this career, we see the opportunity to change the lives of our children. In the younger years of life, there is an insatiable desire for learning. Children are so curious. They want to know the answer to the unanswerable question of why. As teachers we realize that we have the opportunity to shape the future, because we hold in our hands the very moldable thoughts and emotions of the young child. We not only give them knowledge and the love for learning, but we also form their character. We design their morals, and pour the foundation for their future.

The book of Proverbs says to *"Train up a child in the way he should go: and when he is old, he will not depart from it."* (Proverbs 22:6). While we know that this verse is speaking of spiritual influences, it also lets us know that we are responsible for instilling the right morals and values into the minds of our children. Politics tell us to vote for this one or that one to change the direction of the world. The politicians have actually convinced themselves that they are the ones who can change the future. However, it is teachers who have the power to change the direction of our world by changing the children. One Pope made the claim that if you will give him your child for the first five years of his or her life, they would be a Catholic for life. It is in the early years, through the educational process that the path of life is formed. This is why we teach. We know we can make a difference, and we want to make that difference.

One of my former students (we will call her Rita) called my office some time back. She was discouraged at her job working with preschool children. I will never forget the question she posed that day. "As one of your students, do you really think I am cut out to be a teacher?" After less than a year in the classroom, she was thinking about quitting. Why would she be in this shape? She had always demonstrated a great ability to teach and more importantly, a great love for children. I knew that her frustration was coming from the stress of her job, and the fact that she had lost her focus on the big picture.

As we continued to talk, I asked Rita why she wanted to be a teacher in the first place. Her reply was the typical "I wanted to make a difference" answer. Finally, out of nowhere, I instructed her to tell me about one of her students. Without a pause, she began to tell me about this little girl (let's call her Amanda) that was so precious in her class. It seems that Amanda had it a little harder at home. In the mornings, it was necessary to give her a bath before allowing her to play with the other children. Rita, however, made a connection with this girl, and every day little Amanda runs to her for a hug. She wants to play with Rita all of the time. She has begun to flourish under the care of this wonderful teacher. My words to her were that you wanted to make a difference. I think you are making a difference in Amanda's life. The change was immediate. Stress melted away. She said, "I have never thought of it that way. You are right." Rita has since moved to a different facility, but she is still making a difference in children's lives.

The problem here is that we get so overwhelmed with the repetitive nature of this career. Something is always happening, and it seems that we never get a break to go our way. When we get so focused on all of the problems we are facing every day, we forget about the difference we are making for our Amanda. We get so uptight; we never notice that in the middle of our frantic stress, there is a tiny life that is begging us for love and guidance. I guarantee that it would not take over a moment for each of you to think of an Amanda that you have touched. No doubt, you have many Amandas. You have just been focusing on the problems, instead of the successes.

Scripture shows us how easily this can happen. The story is about a visit Jesus made to a couple of sisters. I am sure they felt that this was a great honor to have such an esteemed guest. Along with the Master, many others came to meet and hear such a wonderful teacher. Preparations were needed. Martha, one of the sisters, realized that this was a very important visit, and she wanted everything to be perfect. So she frantically runs around peeling potatoes, frying chicken, making pies, washing dishes, and whatever else needed to be done to make sure all of the guests were comfortable. Luke 10:40 says, *"But Martha was cumbered about much serving."* She wanted Jesus to make Mary come help her. Remember, there were so many things that *had* to be done.

As teachers, we feel the pressure to take care of many responsibilities that seem very important to us and our administrators. We have deadlines, paperwork, and even certain standards we are obligated to teach in a very short time. We become cumbered by it. This word literally means that we are hindered, hampered, or overly burdened by something. We become so engrossed in all of the "other" duties that we are kept from doing the most important. What are we hindered from doing? We are failing to do the very thing that is needful.

Jesus answered Martha with a soft rebuke. *"Martha, Martha, thou art careful and troubled about many things. But one thing is needful: and Mary hath chosen that good part, which shall not be taken away from her."* (Luke 10:41-42). Mary remembered that there was something more important than cooking and cleaning. Sure all of that needed to be done, but hearing Jesus was so much more vital at the moment. Jesus may never come by her house again. She may never have the opportunity to learn from Him again. Household chores will be there every day, but He may not be. The same focus needs to be on our classes. We have one opportunity to touch the lives of these children. Next year, they will move on. Our chance to make a difference will be gone. The paperwork will still be there, but that precious soul will not be. We have to choose that needful thing.

I remember a boy in my second grade class. Drake was definitely one hundred percent boy. He was rambunctious, playful, and full of energy. I was warned about him by his first grade teacher. He was going to tear up my class, and with him in my class, we would never get anything accomplished. As a matter of fact, I was asked by administration if they could place him in my class, simply because I was a man and he might respond to me better than he had to previous teachers. I agreed only with the stipulation that I be allowed to handle his discipline without interference from the front office. (Don't get scared: My plans did not include electroshock or any such abusive actions. Too often, administration is overloaded with "situations", so they choose quick fixes to problems. These include quick suspensions or medication. I cannot help a child who is at home or drugged out of his mind.) I must quickly admit to the fact that Drake and I did have our run-ins. As I would talk with his mother about discipline problems, she would ask if I thought he needed to be on medicine. It seemed that this idea had been suggested to her as the best way to "control" him. Every time she asked I would reply that I believed he was just an active second grade boy, and that I was willing to work with him if she would trust me.

Throughout the year, it became evident that Drake's actions were nothing more than a cry for attention. He was not trying to be arrogant. He was not trying to be a defiant brat. He was simply a young kid in need of someone to show him they cared. Let me add here that his mother was doing all she could to give him that attention, but as is the case in so many single parent families, she was stretched thin and needed help. Sometimes his actions would be so severe that I would have to use conventional discipline with him, but mostly I tried to just take up time with him. I made an attempt to talk with him and more importantly, let him talk to me. As I gave him positive attention, he began to respond. Shortly after Christmas break a P.E. teacher pulled me to the side and asked what was wrong with Drake. Drake had constantly been the cause of problems during P.E., but the discipline problems had almost disappeared. Many days Drake would even come sit by me at recess just to talk. Even the principal asked me about him, because he was never in the office anymore. One of the hardest things I have ever done was to say goodbye to Drake that year, because he was changing schools, and I had no idea what awaited him in the third grade. I kept wondering who would be willing to take up that precious time with him.

A few years later I ran into his mother. I had to fight the tears as she told her friends that I was the only teacher who cared enough about her son to work with him. According to her, everyone else did not have the time to be bothered and just advised her to put

Drake on medicine. Then she told me that perhaps because of me, he is now a disciplined young man, doing well in school, and playing football with the local school team. However, the highlight of this story came just a few months later when a handsome young man walked up to me in Wal-Mart, looked me in the eyes with respect, and held out his hand for a shake. That, my friends, is why we go into teaching. That is the needful thing. That is the good part. I feel as though I really made a difference in a little boy's life.

Did the change in Drake's life continue? Just a couple of weeks ago, I was privileged to assist a local high school with a program dealing with some of the peer pressure our teens are facing in school. In one group of six, a young man suddenly blurted out that he knew me. It was Drake! He is completing ninth grade, still playing sports, and proudly sporting A's and B's on his report cards. Does he still have a mischievous glint in his eyes? Absolutely! Did he give me the impression that he would pull a prank given the chance? Yes he did! But he also carried the air of respect that is missing in so many of our young people's lives. He had the signs of a young man who was going places in life. That is what matters.

Each of you could tell story after story just like this. You could tell of the students that were shy, under-achievers, and yet because of your love for them, they have become leaders on the cheer squad, or captains of the football team. Some may be in college. Some may be raising their own families now. Others may be the business and industry leaders of our communities. Sure, it is possible they could have made it without you. But it would have been a whole lot harder for them. You made the difference.

The fact is this. It is time to remember why you got into teaching anyway. You have to remember and once again choose that good part. If you do not, you are going to stress yourself out of a very rewarding career. So, the next time you feel like you are swamped with mounds of paperwork, just think: paperwork does not change lives, teachers do. At your next IEP meeting, remind yourself that an IEP does not create a better learner, you do. When the 504 plan is not working, please understand that a 504 plan cannot changes minds, but a teacher can. All of the tiers of intervention in the world will not shape the morals and ethics of a young child. It is you that will make that difference. When you are so stressed about the faculty meeting, just remember: faculty meetings do not make a child's life better, but you do. These "other" things are important and have to be done, but they are not the good part.

The first step in overcoming the stress in your career is to loosen up. Forget about those things you cannot change. They will always be there. You will have to do them no matter what happens to your students. So do not worry about them. Do not let paperwork control you. Do not let new standards get you down. The faculty meetings are just part of the job. The changes in your students are your career. No, it is your calling. You only have those little ones in your grasp for a second. You have that one moment in time to stop and make the difference for a child. That should be your focus, because that one life is what you can change. Loosen up!

Teachers must remember that in each school year and in each new classroom, students will walk in with their dreams spread open before us. Too many times, the adults in their lives crush their hopes without ever considering the consequences of doing so. You are the one that can encourage that young person to go for those dreams. This should be our goal. Focus not on the aggravation of the job, but rather choose the good part. Find your Drakes. Find your Amandas. Start working to make a difference in the lives of every child that God places in your path, and your stress level will begin to come down.

Chapter Four
Lighten Up!

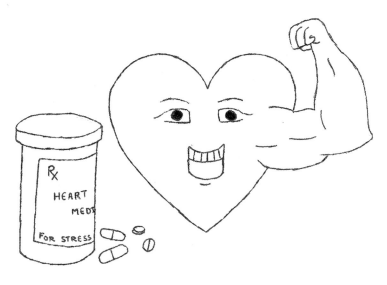

The Strength of a Merry Heart

The next step in combating your stress is to lighten up. In the previous chapter, we discussed the possibility of being so uptight that we forget the big picture. Once we get focused back on our true calling and desire, we now have to lighten up. Proverbs 17:22 says, "*A merry heart doeth good like a medicine. . .*" The wisest man to ever live knew that with all of life's troubles, we have to have humor to survive. I have heard it said that it takes about sixty or seventy muscles in our face to frown. On the other hand, it only takes about seven to smile. If this is true, some of us are working ourselves to death.

So in the midst of all the pressures of a classroom, how can one have a merry heart? First of all, we must remember that children are funny. I know what you are thinking. Their little antics can be annoying, and certainly disrupt the perfect plan you had for your day, but you have to admit, they are funny. I have come to realize that most of the time children are not trying to be disrespectful. Neither are they challenging your authority as their teacher. The majority of the time, they are simply being children, and children are funny.

First, if you haven't already discovered this truth, children are innocently honest. This means they will tell you everything without reserve. Mothers and fathers would be aghast to know what their child is telling teachers about them at school. They have been taught to tell the truth, so they tell the truth. Children cannot differentiate between truth that should be told and truth that is better left untold. This innocent honesty is sometimes hilarious. If we could just take some of these outrageous and shocking statements for what they are (kids being kids), the humor from these incidents would help us to lighten up.

The lesson that day was all about multiple meaning words. I was at the board writing words as my second grade class called them out. As I wrote each word, I would ask a student for the first definition and then another student for a different definition. The activity was going smoothly. It was one of those days when everything was going right. Then an innocent second grader calls out the word "moon"! What do I do now? Teachers know that research shows we should use students' suggestions as much as possible to foster the feelings of importance and acceptance. So, since I have a great sense of humor, I turned and wrote "moon" on the board.

Of course, the first definition to be given to me was the big white light in the sky at night. "That is a great job, little one! Now, who knows another definition for the word moon?" I was ready to squelch any problems that might arise. Sure enough, the answer came: "It is when you . . . well, you know." I quickly look at my "BAD" kids. There was no response. It was a miracle. I breathed a sigh of relief and turned to write another word on the board, when suddenly, the innocent honesty of a little girl shows up. "My mama does that all the time," she blurted out. Unfortunately for me, this event took place just a few days before parent/teacher conferences.

Was that too much information? Of course it was. Should the girl have said that? Of course not. Would her mother be mortified if she knew her daughter said that? Of course she would be. Is this something that I as a teacher should be concerned about? Well, I could get uptight about it and stress about it. However, even the most serious of you reading this will have to admit: that was FUNNY! I think I will choose to see the humor and lighten up.

Another incident occurred following Christmas break one year. Being the very unique and imaginative teacher that I am, I came up with the best journal writing activity that has ever been created. "This morning class, I want you to write in your journals about something you did over the holidays." Now that was creative, wasn't it? As the students began writing, I noticed a small boy that was more involved and focused than he had ever been. He, a boy who usually writes about one paragraph, was writing furiously. One page turned to two pages, and then the third page materialized. I could not wait to read what had happened during Christmas. Soon I experienced a story unlike any I had ever read.

The writing told a story of imagination, horror, and even danger.

This young man had hosted a sleep-over at his house. He named several of his friends in the class as those who were visiting. As they were playing that evening, they were suddenly attacked by a ferocious monster. They fought and fought with this monster, but he kept pushing them back and pushing them back. It soon became obvious that the monster was going to win the fight and eat them all! Suddenly, thinking quickly, this second grader comes up with a plan and after giving me a very graphic description, saves the day.

My readers may review this story looking for the humor and wonder what is funny about it. The humor is in the one detail I have left out until now. You see, this little boy was having trouble with his spelling. As a result, throughout the entire writing, he misspelled a word, turning it into a curse word. At first, I could not believe what I was seeing. As an adult, I had a choice. As a teacher, I had a choice. Even worse, as a minister, I had a choice. I could get uptight and stressed, wondering what this world is coming to when little boys write such "bad" things. I could discipline him for using inappropriate words in his journal. I could call mom in and embarrass her with the insinuation that he is learning curse words at home. I could lose it, and cause my stress level to rise to great proportions.

On the other hand, I could choose to lighten up. This incident was actually hilarious. Of course I am not saying that a little boy using "bad" words is funny, but it was so obvious that this second grade boy had no idea he was misspelling a word and cursing on three pages of his journal. He was simply a little boy trying to tell an exciting and imaginative story about an adventure with his friends. I could choose to find the humor in this and let the laughter wash away the stress of the day. I could realize that kids make funny errors and we should treat them as such. My choice was to lighten up. After laughing for a while, I called him in and explained his mistake to him. Then, I laminated the writing and gave it to his mother and told her to give it to his wife on their wedding day.

I think I have made the point well that children are funny. However, kids are not the only ones that are funny. Adults can be quite hilarious as well. We make crazy mistakes all of the time. The problem is we get embarrassed when we say something "stupid" or do something "foolish." Why? We are quick to say that everyone makes mistakes and that the occasional mistake is okay, but this is just as long as it happens with someone else. We try to portray the image that we are totally perfect and never could we be found to have a flaw.

This desire to have that perfect image, especially as professionals, is taking us to new and higher stress levels. We will not admit that we are human. The fact is only one man ever walked on this Earth who could claim to be perfect. None of us can say that we are called Jesus Christ, the Son of God. Therefore, no matter how hard we try, we are going to make mistakes. The good part is most of these mistakes are absolutely hilarious. The way we treat them will control to some extent the levels of our stress.

I was a new pastor. I had only been in my position for a couple of weeks, and was just learning the congregation's names. Full of zeal and excitement, I wanted to impress the members each time I stood in the pulpit. In one fateful service, God seemed to be moving in a great way. Being Pentecostal, I was thrilled as two sisters began to be blessed during our choir service. I also was glad that I knew their names. This was Sister Virginia and Sister Pat. I could not wait to get to the podium. I began to exhort the church: "I really appreciate the Lord coming by and moving. I thank Him for coming by and blessing Sister Virginia and Sister Fat like that!" No, that is not a typo. Yes, I said it. What do you do? You suffer that moment of intense embarrassment; thank the Good Lord above that she is not actually fat, and then laugh hysterically over your mistake.

Just the other day, I entered my classroom, glanced at the students, saw that all seats were filled, and proceeded to begin my lesson. Quickly I reviewed the last few notes from my previous lecture, and launched into the day's topic. You must understand me when I say, I love my job. Lecturing to a class full of attentive students is my favorite thing to do. Needless to say, I was enjoying myself as I imparted my wisdom to these brains in front of me. However, it was not long before I noticed they were not really taking notes, nor did they seem to be getting anything from my speech. In fact, they appeared to be quite confused. It was when I stopped to inquire of the problem that I discovered I was lecturing to the wrong class. Oh it was the right *classroom*, but the wrong class. I was so embarrassed, and probably would never have told the story here. But something happened a few days later that totally changed my outlook on the situation. I was talking with a group of people when one, also a college teacher, told us of going into the wrong classroom and beginning her lecture. She saw the humor in it and was laughing as she was telling the story. I decided then to lighten up. It was rather funny anyway, and my students are still laughing about it.

I remember a neighboring teacher as she was planning to show a movie to her class. Unfortunately, she could not get the VCR to play the video. The TV would not even come on. No matter what she tried, nothing would come on. For about thirty minutes she worked, becoming very frustrated in the process. Finally, she gave up and called for the media specialist. This expert walked into the classroom, plugged the TV and VCR up, and believe it or not, the crazy contraption started playing. Now that was so embarrassing for the teacher. We laughed for weeks about it. No, maybe it was not very professional, but it was definitely funny. Come on, lighten up!

Think about the crazy mistakes you have made. Were they embarrassing? I have done such crazy things before that I literally avoided my coworkers and friends. The problem is that avoidance does not change the fact that I made a silly mistake. In fact, the longer I dwell on it, and try to forget it, the more it controls me. So, what have I found to be the answer? I admit to myself that I can make some of the stupidest mistakes that have ever been made. Then I make myself realize that the only harm from my mistakes is a little bruising of my pride. Finally, the sooner I lighten up, the sooner it is all over. After all, most of the time our mistakes are hilarious.

They say that there are two sides to every coin. For those of us who are so stressed out, choosing the right side may be the difference in us losing our mind or keeping our sanity. One side of the teaching coin contains all of those annoying things that happen day by day. Whether it is the children doing crazy things, or we as adults making silly mistakes, this side shows us all of the negative results of whatever has happened. The other side shows us the same events, but with a twist. On this side, we can see the hilarity. On this side, we can laugh and even enjoy the awkward moments. The good news is we do not have to flip the coin to see which side will come up. We have the right to choose which side we would rather have.

Finding humor in the day's activities will go a long ways toward relieving the tension and stress you are experiencing. Life is too short to spend it worrying about making everything happen perfectly. Let us conclude that we are going to have troubles. We have a choice as to how we will react to them. One elderly minister was counseling a young pastor. The pastor was going through a hard time with his first church. As he was sharing his burden, his troubles, and his fears with the elder, to his chagrin the older man started laughing. With his feelings hurt, he asked the man why he would laugh after hearing all of the troubles. The wise elder replied, "You might as well laugh as cry."

A merry heart really does do you good like a medicine! Look back at what has you so stressed out. Can you find any humor in the situation at all? If so, focus on that. Laugh through your tears. Remember, this too shall pass. Take your merry medicine and lighten up.

Chapter Five
Look Up!

So now we have loosened up and lightened up. We are well into our journey of living a much less stressful life. However, stressful things will still take place. All too often, professionals "bottle" these events up until they reach an exploding point which cannot be controlled. This works much like a pressure cooker. The steam builds and builds on the inside. Finally, the pot can take no more, so it begins to blast out with amazing power. Humans react much the same way. The outside appearance seems to be just fine. We try to give the impression that we are calm, cool, and collected. Then, suddenly, for no apparent reason, we snap. We detonate with a fury, without a chance of controlling our actions. It is too bad that usually our loved ones are the ones who take the brunt of our meltdown.

We cannot stop with loosening up and lightening up. We also have to look up. There are two ways we have to do this. David said, *"I will lift up mine eyes unto the hills, from whence cometh my help. My help cometh from the Lord, which made heaven and earth."* (Psalm 121:1-2). This great psalmist knew there would be times when he could not handle things on his own. He had to surrender his feelings and emotions to the One who could give him the strength to make it another day.

I know a man who is a pastor of great character. His reputation is that he is a tremendous man of God. Yet his own testimony tells of a time when stress almost took him out of the ministry. Finally he made the decision to go to a dear friend's house, along with his wife. Once there, he told his friend that he just needed to kneel down beside his couch and cry out to God like he was not even saved. You may say that is foolishness, but this pastor stated that he was on the verge of losing his mind and was willing to do whatever it took to get in touch with his God. The result: he looked to the hills and received his help. He is still pastoring today and doing a great work in his community.

What about those of us in the teaching profession? Sometimes we find ourselves in situations that we cannot share with anyone. The laws of confidentiality force us to hold everything in and smile. How many times have you longed for someone you could run to and just unload your burden and your heartbreak on them? Instead, you cried yourself to sleep worried about little Johnny. Can I share with you that there is one that can listen without you being worried about breaking any laws? As I have mentioned before, He invites us to, "*Come unto me, all ye that labour and are heavy laden and I will give you rest. Take my yoke upon you, and learn of me; for I am meek and lowly in heart: and ye shall find rest unto your souls. For my yoke is easy, and my burden light*" (Matthew 11:28 – 30).

Obviously, there is a lot more to teaching than most people ever see. Not only do teachers have the privilege of working with precious little children, but they also have the opportunity to impart to those same boys and girls the knowledge and wisdom that they will need to succeed in life. If that were all that the job required, there would be no stress. However, there is another aspect that the public cannot and will not see. Teachers also get to know their students. Information is given about their fears, their home lives, their struggles, and their failures. The teacher becomes a mentor and a counselor for many. As the burden of knowing the problems and situations of the students pile up, where does the teacher turn? Who does the teacher talk with? Where can we go to confide in someone?

I had the privilege of working in an elementary school whose student population was largely made up of poverty level or lower kids. These families lived in trailers with no windows and doors. Some had no siding, and you could literally see the insulation in the walls. Sometimes, you could even see through the walls! Each year, the teachers would take a bus tour through the neighborhood, so we could get a close glimpse of the socioeconomic status our students were coming from. A study was done by some well-meaning government agency, and this community was ranked lower than a third world country.

These precious kids came from homes with drugs being sold from the front steps. Sometimes they were not sure if they could even go home or not. Several of their homes have no heating or air conditioning. Many do not even have running water. Open sewage runs from under a few of the trailers. No, this is not in a foreign country. This is right here in the United States of America.

The teachers at this school did and still do a miraculous job of helping these children. However, sometimes the best efforts do not seem to be enough. I remember a little boy who came to my class each day with a pair of shoes that were little more than a few scraps of cloth. We had a clothing closet, full of clothes that had been donated by the community, so this boy received a new pair of shoes. The next day he came to school with the scraps on his feet. When asked about the new shoes, he replied, "My daddy sold them." My stress level went out of the roof. Stress can definitely be brought on by anger.

What can one do in this situation? DEFACS is swamped with cases from this area. Their caseload has them so far behind that unless the child is in immediate danger, it will be weeks and even months before they can check on this child. Certainly a teacher cannot do what they want to do. Impulse says to find the dad and teach him a thing or two about being a father. Please refer at this time to the second definition of stress found in chapter one! Unfortunately, all we could do was have him shoes to wear during the school day, and then give him the rags back to wear home.

My first Christmas with these children added to my stress as well. I was working as a Paraprofessional in a Kindergarten class. We were excited to be having a traditional Christmas party in our class. It was great! The lead teacher had purchased all of the little boys and girls two gifts each, and I had purchased them one each. There was so much excitement as the children tore open their gifts to find the stuffed animal and book from their teacher, as well as a tractor (for the boys) and a doll (for the girls) from their Para-pro. Then I saw him. One little boy, standing to the side, was watching his classmates with so much joy in his eyes, but his three gifts remained unopened.

I walked over and knelt beside my student. He held up an unwrapped gift, looked around at the others, and said, "Look Mr. Taft. I have a stuffed whale." He patted another and said, "Look Mr. Taft. I have a book." Then, with more excitement, he held up my gift, completely wrapped, and said, "Look Mr. Taft. I have a tractor." Not understanding, I encouraged him to go ahead and open his gifts, but he would not take a peep. After a few moments, I asked him why he would not open his presents. His reply brought tears to my eyes and my heart broke as I realized his dilemma. He said, "No Mr. Taft. I want to take them home and put them under my tree." In that instant, I understood why he was keeping his gifts intact. He had no gifts at home. There was going to be no Christmas morning celebration at his house. But this kindergartener was forced by circumstances to choose between opening his three gifts now and having three gifts under the tree for Christmas morning. All I could do was wrap him a great big bear hug and tell him that it was okay. Of course he could take his gifts home if that was what he wanted.

In another school two Hispanic boys came to us late in the fall of the year. They were twins, and were the cutest young men you have ever seen. Administration placed them in the second grade because of their age. There were no records to speak of. The few records they had displayed sporadic school attendance ranging from Mexico to Texas to Florida. One of them was placed in my class, and the other was in the room across the hall. From the beginning it was plain to see that there was a "situation" concerning these two.

They were definitely behind in academics, but that was not the problem. The difficulty was the fear expressed by them throughout the day. Each constantly wanted to cross the hall to check on his brother. The mother did not want them out of our sight at any time. We were finally told that they were on the run from an abusive dad. He would get arrested, but soon would post bail and be back, abusing and tormenting them. Their life was a living nightmare. After a while it appeared that they had escaped the dad. They began to flourish. It was apparent they were brilliant students. We were making such great progress with them, when one day the unthinkable happened.

A well-meaning aunt told the father where his wife and children were hiding. With no chance to say good-bye to their classmates or teachers, these boys were once again uprooted and moved to a location unknown. That morning, we were told to pack anything that belonged to them and deliver it to the office. We were not allowed to see them or have any contact with them. No one ever told us if they were okay or not. I cried. Seven years later and I still worry about them.

There are stories after stories teachers could tell. But who can they tell them to? Who can understand the stress of situations like this? What about the kid who announces to the class that he did not get any sleep last night, because his daddy got arrested again for D.U.I.? What about the child whose parents are going through a nasty divorce and she cries off and on all day? What about the student who runs to her mother and hugs her as though her life depends on it, yet you can't let her go, because dad has a restraining order against mom? Who do you tell about these cases?

Teachers may hide their soft hearts behind a calloused exterior, but rest assured they care. I am a tough old man, but I have cried about my "babies" many times through the years. We go into teaching because we care. Our problem is that sometimes our care is not cared for, and this leads to tremendous pressure in our hearts and minds. If we do not find an outlet for this stress in God, we will soon face the nervous breakdowns and career ending burnout. There is only one place to go. There is only one who understands. You have to go down on your knees so that you can lift your eyes to the hills. He has invited you to cast all of your cares on Him. Take Him up on the offer. Only God can comfort you and relieve that stress.

There is also a second part to looking up. Sometimes, as stressed as we get, God is not enough. Wait a minute! Don't tie me to a stake and burn me as a heretic yet! Listen to what I have to say. It is not that God is powerless and for some reason cannot comfort us. On the contrary, God gives us tremendous access to His glory and might! His servant Paul even tells us to *". . . come boldly unto the throne of grace, that we may obtain mercy, and find grace to help in time of need."* (Hebrews 4:16). This seems to indicate that He is there for us at all times.

Well, He is, but sometimes He chooses other methods to give us relief. In His infinite wisdom, He purposely created us with a built in need for others. We have an innate desire to have close relationships with other humans. Therefore, not only should we depend on God for our help, we should also turn to those He has placed in our lives at this time.

David again makes a proclamation in a stressful time. *"From the end of the earth will I cry unto thee, when my heart is overwhelmed: lead me to the rock that is higher than I"* (Psalm 61:2). He is praying to God, but as his heart gets so stressed, he calls to someone in whom he has upmost confidence. He says, "Hey friend, I am overwhelmed at the moment. I am so stressed that I can't seem to get to God by myself. I am blinded by the pressure and in danger of losing my way. Please, help me get back to the rock."

To fight the stress in our lives, we not only need to pray and seek God, but we need to have a network of friends that we can run to for help. These need to be strong and steadfast men or women of God. They must be towers that you can lean on when you are weak. They must be wise in their counsel, so they will always listen and then point you back to the rock. These towers of faith that God has placed in your life cannot be novices. They must have the experience to be able to guide you. They must be trustworthy. No backbiters, gossipers, or talebearers need apply for this position.

I would advise that this person, or these people, be someone outside of your immediate family. Your family needs you at your best. Your spouse does not deserve to be laden down with every problem that you have. On top of that, if your spouse loves you, he or she cannot be objective when listening to your pain. No, this must be someone who can listen without judgment and give Godly advice no matter the circumstance. So, put the book down and go find this person that you can trust to be there for you. I will wait for you.

Okay, you are back, so you must have found someone. But finding them is not enough. You have to reach an agreement with them. You have to commit to "unloading" on them on a regular basis. Without this help, you can never get free from the stress that has been overtaking you. The good thing is, your friend or mentor does not have to do anything besides listen. Sometimes they may offer advice as the Lord leads, but mainly they are just an ear to hear, and a shoulder to lean on. Most of all, they will recognize when your heart is becoming overwhelmed. When that time comes, they will lead you to the Rock. They will take you to the stability of God. They will help you to once again be strong in the Lord They will help you to look up!

Chapter Six
Let Go!

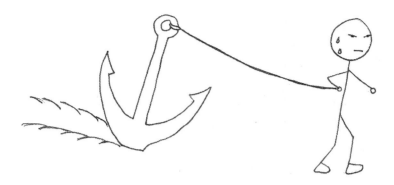

This Anchor of Stress is Holding Me Back

The fourth and final leg of your journey to low or no stress is perhaps the hardest of them all. No doubt you have been through many trials during your excursion as a teacher. Some of those tests may have left you with bitterness and hardness in your heart. The problem is that stress is always compounded by the memories of things that have happened in your past. You have to let go. Although you have made it through the hardships and worries of days gone by, the feelings and emotions caused by difficult times grow. They continue to build on the inside until your love of life slowly starts to die. You have no choice but to let go.

We hold the Apostle Paul in very high esteem. He is arguably the most powerful preacher of the New Testament Church. However, we cannot forget that this great man of God did not have a ministry of ease. Remember, when he first came to our attention? He was a persecutor of the church. His sole purpose in life was to arrest, prosecute, and torment or even kill the followers of Christ. He was a murderer who gave the consent for the execution of Stephen. He even gave the witness of himself that he was the chief among sinners. How could anyone with this testimony be anything for Christ?

After he became converted and his name was changed from Saul to Paul, his difficulties really began. Among the many things he suffered, we find that he was beaten by the Jews (his own people) five times with thirty nine stripes. Three times he was beaten with rods, one time he was stoned and left for dead, and three different times he was shipwrecked in his travels. II Corinthians 11:24 – 28 continues on to tell of him being in the sea for a day and night. In verse 27 he talks of being weary, in pain, hungry, thirsty, and even cold and naked. This is a man who is familiar with troubles.

Take a moment and look at verse 26 for a moment. It speaks of all kinds of perils that he found himself in throughout his ministry. However, two of those really caught my attention. Paul says, "In perils by my own countrymen" and "In perils among false brethren." Do you understand what he is saying? My own people did this! My own loved ones hurt me! Those whom I considered my brothers in the faith, turned against me, and I suffered because of it. These are the ones I counted on the most, and they proved to be my foremost tormentors.

That is what stresses us the most. We seem to have everything going just right, but a friend or a loved one does us wrong. The fact that it came from the last possible person we would expect it from multiplies the pain. Our administrators seem to turn their back after we have worked so hard for them (Granted, they may not have had a choice, but during the trial, we can't see that). We were never rewarded for our faithfulness to the school or to the children, but we made that one mistake, and everyone made sure we suffered for it. The friends we once leaned on for strength, now seem to shun us. Those who were our greatest allies are now trying to tear us down.

Too often, this hurt eats away at our heart until it begins to control us. We wake in the mornings dreading the day of work because of the feelings of betrayal. We would rather not face those who have caused us this pain. The very ones we have trusted are the ones who are the source of our anger. For weeks we tiptoe around the facts, until it seems to be under control. Then, about the time we think we have gotten free from the past, some random words are spoken that rip open old wounds and memories come flooding back in. Anger and hurt that we thought we had put behind us washes over us again, and we feel despair. We are controlled by it!

This is the kind of pain Paul experienced. He was betrayed by the ones he most loved! So how does this man who has been done so wrong continue on to eventually become such a powerful preacher for the New Testament Church? He explains this to us in his epistle to the church in Philippi. His strategy for coping with all that had happened to him was this: *"Brethren, I count not myself to have apprehended: but this one thing I do, forgetting those things which are behind, and reaching forth unto those things which are before, I press toward the mark for the prize of the high calling of God in Christ Jesus."* (Philippians 3: 13 – 14). What is he saying here? "Folks, I have not made it yet. I am still on my journey. I know that many things have happened to get me down, but I also know that if I am going to make it, I have to forget about those things in my past. The only important thing is for me to keep going on. I have a goal, and I am going to press towards it. I will not let what others have done to me stop me from making it."

I have heard many make the comment that "I forgive them, but I will never forget!" While we can understand that statement, does holding on to the bad memories actually constitute forgiveness? All too often, we operate on the treasure map system. We go as far as to bury the hatchet, but before we leave the graveyard, we draw a detailed map with directions on how to find it! We buried it, but "X" marks the spot! At any given time, even years later, we can go back and dig up the old anger and hatred. Until we let it go, until we tear up the map, we will never be free from the control of things that should be left in the past.

There is absolutely nothing you can do about those things in the past. Although many movies have been made about time travel, you cannot go back. Therefore, you have to make a choice. You can continue to relive those things of the past, or you can simply let it go. The consequences of each are vastly different. To continue to hold on to the hurt and hard feelings will add to the stress of your everyday lives. They will control you and your actions. Also, as the feelings remain, they will grow. They will build until you are overcome with bitterness. If you choose to let the past go, you will give your heart the freedom to enjoy life. Healing will take place and your stress dissipates.

If you want to take this step and let go, you will have to call in FIDO. FIDO is a good "dog" who has helped me out of many potential stress filled emotional breakdowns. Who is FIDO? He is just a simple acronym that stands for "Forget It and Drive On!" That's what Paul was saying. He does not have time to worry about yesterday, so he will forget it. There is so much to look forward to and to work for, so he is going to drive on. This simple strategy will become priceless if you will put it into practice.

I do know that we actually cannot blank out things that are in our memories. So forgetting is really just a choice. I choose to leave it in the past where it belongs. Remember, Satan takes notes of everything you do, and everything that has been done to you. He will try to sidetrack you by reminding you of the past. He will drag it up at the most inopportune times. I have been in the pulpit delivering a sermon when he sidled up to me and asked, "Why are you even up here? Remember *this* from your past? You do not even qualify to minister God's Word with that on your record."

This used to bother me. Then I was present when someone tried to bring up the past of one of the Godliest men I have ever known; my father-in-law. This person was trying to hurt my wife's family, and decided to do it by sullying the reputation of her father. Some in her family were really upset by these accusations, but Mr. Aubrey was never shaken. He simply stated to everyone, "That was a long time ago, and it is under the Blood." That settled it. FIDO. How can we let it go? We put it under the Blood of Jesus, and because of this, the past no longer has control over us.

There is another aspect of letting go that does not deal with hurts and hard feelings. It simply deals with the events of everyday teaching. All teachers find that they will work with certain situations over and over in the classroom. Sometimes it can be students who are a little hyperactive and seem to cause problems all of the time. This can be very discouraging for a teacher. After several weeks, a teacher may get so focused on the negative behavior that he or she begins to dread going to work each day. This causes great amounts of stress. That teacher wakes up thinking about the "bad" student, and wonders what kind of disaster that student will create this day.

I remember a college student I had that was in the middle of her practicum experience. There was a kid in the class that fit the description of constantly bad. One day, the childcare center director called me with some disturbing news. The little boy was late getting to class that day, and my student let it be known she was happy about him being absent. When she saw him as he arrived late, she vocalized her displeasure in a very inappropriate way. In fact, the mother of this child heard her comment. Needless to say, there had to be disciplinary action. Her stress, caused by a kid's daily bad behavior, caused her to receive attention she did not want or need.

So what do you do when you have these children in your class? You have to let it go. This morning is just what it seems to be: a new morning. Yesterday is gone. The problems from then are forever gone. Sure, you will probably have situations today, but they are today's situations. Let yesterday's go. God's grace and mercy comes to us fresh every morning. He gives us a new start. We should do the same with our students. Of course they cause you grief, but it is a new day. Let's try again today. Today may just be the day your "bad" kid gets it right.

Maybe the stressor is not a student. There are many other things that sometimes cause anger and hurt. Perhaps the problem stems from a co-worker. Could it be that an administrator treated you in a way you thought unfair? A parent has possibly talked about you in a negative light. Funding may have been cut again, and furlough days have reappeared. These are things that you cannot change. Remember that and let go.

Situations that are beyond our control too often bring us down. We begin to spend our energy trying to find a solution or a quick fix. We worry and fret about the issue until we find ourselves focusing most of our time on the very problem we can do nothing about. Then we get angry because we are not able to change the predicament. It becomes an obsession that controls us. We know that it shouldn't, but we cannot seem to do anything about it. That cause undue amounts of stress. The only answer is to let go.

My mother is quite possibly the world's number one best worrier! She worries about her children of course, but she also worries about the economy, and the earthquakes, and the storms, and the government, and on and on and on. She does not sleep well sometimes, because of worry and stress. As I was talking with her one evening I asked her, "Does God ever sleep?" Her reply was, "Of course not." I suggested that since He was going to stay up all night, why did she not just go to sleep, get some rest, and let Him worry about things. That is the solution. Let go and let God!

CHAPTER SEVEN
IN CONCLUSION

In the classic novel *A Tale of Two Cities*, written in 1859 by Charles Dickens, the writer begins his story with the famous lines, "It was the best of times. It was the worst of times." One hundred and fifty four years later, I could borrow his phrasing and apply it to our day. Never before have we seen such a marvelous age. The wonders of science and technology abound everywhere we turn. Mankind has made huge advances in medicine and the last couple of generations have witnessed the eradication of some diseases. Heart surgeries are routine occurrences. One can go into the hospital for major treatments and be home the next day. This must be the best of times.

We reached the moon, we are exploring Mars, and humanity watches on their televisions, cell phones, and laptop computers. The average automobile has more computer power than NASA had just a few short years ago. Satellites track children, and their parents know where they are at all times, simply by glancing at the phone. Enormous amounts of data can be stored on a flash drive which is small enough to get lost in your pocket. Entire books can be downloaded instantly onto a tablet for reading pleasure. Yes, it must be the best of times!

On the other hand, it is also the worst of times. These advances have obviously forced us to live in a much faster paced society. There are so many wonders out there, and we want to try them all. We must do it all. We have to see it all. As we live this more frantic pace, our stress level rises higher and higher. With that in mind, it is the worst of times. Instead of planning for retirement and leisure, time is spent packing every waking moment with too many things that have to be done. The drive to accomplish so much in such a short period of time brings on the worry. The worry brings on frets and fears. Before long, these turn into pure stress. It is the worst of times.

We have to go back. I am definitely not saying to go back to the days of horse and buggies. Living in South Georgia, I would rather not go back to not having air conditioning. However, we have to go back to a less stressful time. We have to get our lives back under control. Our priorities have to be rearranged. Are all of these modern "things" really that important? Do I really need the newest convenience? Is it so important that I can justify taking on a second or third job, just to keep up with everyone else? What is really important?

Ultimately, the problem stems from within. Our stress is a direct result of a heart issue. I know some will argue that their stress comes from circumstances that cannot be controlled. I understand that argument completely. However, I also know that when our heart is not in the right place, those uncontrollable situations cause great stress. Okay, I have to explain. This is because I have spent an entire book giving you four steps to less stress, and now I conclude by saying it has always been a heart problem. I know that is confusing to say the least. So let me take a few moments to end by appealing to your heart.

First, I will give you one of the most used (or should I say misused) promises in God's word. *"And we know that all things work together for good to them that love God, to them who are the called according to his purpose"* (Romans 8:28). We spout this promise every time something bad happens to someone, but do we really believe it? Do we have the confidence that no matter what is going on, it is going to come together for the good of God's children? We sure don't act like it. We panic. We go into "gotta figure this out" mode. Then, when we cannot change the situation, we get stressed. Where is our faith? What if I could reach out in faith to trust God in all aspects of my life?

Next, we move down to verse 37 in Romans 8. *"Nay, in all these things we are more than conquerors through him that loved us."* I am a conqueror? I am the one who can overcome any obstacle that comes my way. Isn't this what God's Word is saying? Then why does every bump in the road get me so distressed? Each time Satan yells, "Boo!" I cower in fear. I need to readjust my heart. God said I am a conqueror. It is time for me to stop being so stressed about daily troubles and simply trust Him to help me conquer them.

Another heart changing verse is found in Philippians 4:13. *"I can do all things through Christ which strengtheneth me."* All that we have discussed in the previous chapters will overwhelm us. We begin to feel as though we just cannot accomplish the tasks that are set before us. We are behind on every project, and never seem to get caught up. Finally, the stress gets to us and we give up. What about faith? Do I believe that I can do it if Christ strengthens me? Will my heart change and power me through the stress? It will only if I put my full trust in God.

Finally, let's draw everything together for the last word. We have loosened up, lightened up, looked up, and let go. Our stress level may be coming down. We may be feeling some relief. So, what is left? The wisest man who has ever lived may have some advice for us. If we want to be happy and stress free, Solomon says, *"Let us hear the conclusion of the whole matter: Fear God, and keep his commandment: for this is the whole duty of man."* (Ecclesiastes 12:13). Trust God with the entirety of your life. Place all you have into His care. Live wholly for Him, and watch your stress level dwindle to nothing.

May God bless you all!

About the Author

Kyle Taft currently works as Program Coordinator for the Early Childhood Care and Education Department of Wiregrass Georgia Technical College. He holds a bachelor's degree in Early Childhood Education from Valdosta State University, and a master's degree in Early Language and Literacy from Walden University. As a state certified teacher, he has taught at the elementary level in Georgia's public school system, as well as now teaching those desiring to become teachers.

As an ordained minister (holding papers with the Calvary Holiness Association), he has pastored for twelve years. After feeling God's leading to resign his pastorate, he currently teaches the young adult Sunday school class at New Corinth Calvary Holiness Church. He also does part-time evangelistic work, ministering where God opens doors.

He is a Georgia certified firefighter, and volunteers with his local rural fire department. He also serves as Chaplain for the Coffee County Fire and Rescue Department. He and his wife, Patty, live with their two daughters in the small community of Wray, Georgia.

NOTES

NOTES

NOTES

NOTES

NOTES

NOTES

NOTES

NOTES

NOTES

NOTES

NOTES

NOTES

NOTES

NOTES

NOTES